Major Prophets Of The Bible, Isaiah, Jeremiah, Ezekiel, Daniel, Lamentations:

Bible Study Aid - Summary & Commentary On The Old Testament 'Major' Prophets

By

James Paris

Published By

Deanburn Publications

Table of Contents

Contents

Introduction: 1
Isaiah: 4
Jeremiah: 11
Ezekiel: 16
Daniel: 21
Lamentations: 28

Permissions/Copyright

Scripture taken from the NEW AMERICAN STANDARD BIBLE ®,

Copyright © 1960,1962,1963,1968, 1971,1973,1975,1977,1995 by The Lockman Foundation.

Used by permission

Copyright 2022, James Paris

All rights reserved. Copyright protected. Duplicating, reprinting or distributing this material for commercial purposes without the express written consent of the author is prohibited.

While reasonable attempts have been made to assure the accuracy of the information contained within this publication, the author does not assume any responsibility for errors, omissions or contrary interpretation of this information, and any damages incurred by that.

The author does not assume any responsibility or liability whatsoever, for what you choose to do with this information.

www.deanburnpublications.com

www.thebiblebrief.com

Introduction:

Welcome to this brief introduction to the 'Major' prophets of the Bible, as included in the Christian Old Testament.

The Prophets Isaiah, Jeremiah, Ezekiel, and Daniel are the 'big hitters' amongst the Bible prophets and their messages still have a huge impact on the world today. Even though written over 2500 years ago!

The book of Lamentations is also included here, even though in itself Lamentations is a book and not a Prophet – but it is widely acknowledged as being written by the Prophet Jeremiah.

The word 'Major' prophets is used to separate them from the writings of the other 12 prophets of the Bible which come under the title 'Minor' prophets.

This is NOT because the minor prophets are of less importance and their messages 'second rate' far from it! The title 'minor' merely reflects the length of the material as recorded in the bible – which is much shorter than the works of the major prophets.

This complete work is in fact an **expanded version** of the material to be found in the Parent book 'The Bible Brief' which is a summary of the complete 66 books and letters of the Bible from Genesis to Revelation.

More material from The Bible Brief can be found free on our blog https://thebiblebrief.com

The Goal:

As far as commentaries on the Bible Goes, there is definitely no shortage of in-depth studies out there for the serious scholar or Bible student – this is not one of them!

As the title says, this is **an introduction** to these amazing men of God.

As with the other books in the Bible summaries series, this work is intended to introduce the reader to the character and message of the prophet.

Perhaps to inspire further in-depth study when time permits – or The Lord convicts?

I once heard that any sermon or Bible message should make the hearer feel mad, sad, or glad – but it should make them feel something!

With that thought in mind, I have chosen *the passages that spoke to me* as well as factual information such as times, dates, names, etc.

Hopefully this will encourage the reader to go more 'in-depth' and hear what The Lord has to say to them personally, through the writings of these amazing men of God.

The five books are written in the same format as described below.

1. **When:** The date that the book was written or the time period covered.
2. **Who:** The author or presumed author of the book.
3. **People & Places:** The 'main players' & places involved or referred to.
4. **Key Verses:** Memorable quotes, sayings or verses from the book.
5. **The Messianic Link:** The coming Messiah is mentioned throughout – and ties together – the 66 books. These are just some of the scriptures that allude to or name the Messiah directly.
6. **The Book:** An outline of the book or letter.
7. **Notes & Quotes:** General thoughts & comments on the preceding book.

It is my prayer that you will find this brief introductory work to be nevertheless informative, and an inspiration for further study not only of the prophets but the Bible as a whole.

Isaiah:

When:
700 - 680 B.C.

Who:
Isaiah the Prophet (Ch.1:1)

People & Places:
Isaiah; Hezekiah; Cyrus
Judah; Jerusalem; Israel; Moab; Philistia; Assyria; Babylon

Sound-Bites:
"Come now, and let us reason together," Says the Lord, "Though your sins are as scarlet, They will be as white as snow; Though they are red like crimson, They will be like wool." (Ch.1:18)

*"And they will hammer their swords into plowshares and their spears into pruning hooks.
Nation will not lift up sword against nation,
And never again will they learn war." (Ch 2:4)*

*"Therefore the Lord Himself will give you a sign:
Behold, a [a]virgin will be with child and bear a son, and she will call His name [b]Immanuel." (Ch 7:14)*

"For a child will be born to us, a son will be given to us; And the government will rest on His shoulders." (Ch.9:6)

"But He was pierced through for our transgressions,

He was crushed for our iniquities; The chastening for our well-being fell upon Him, And by His scourging we are healed." (Ch.53:5)

*"The Spirit of the Lord GOD is upon me, Because the LORD has anointed me To bring good news to the afflicted;
He has sent me to bind up the broken hearted,
To proclaim liberty to captives And freedom to prisoners."* (Ch 61:1)

The Messianic Link:
The Messiah is typified in several places throughout Isaiah known as the 'Suffering Servant' passages.
In chapter 7 he is born of a virgin (Ch.7:14)
In chapter 9 the messiah would be both God and man (Ch.9:6).

In chapter 35 the Messiah heals the sick (Ch.35:5-6)
He would be rejected by the Jews in chapter 49. (Ch.49:7)
He would be whipped and scourged (Ch.50:6)
Messiah would be the perfect sacrifice (Ch.53)

The Book:
The period of Isaiah's writing covered the reigns of four Judean kings throughout the 8th century B.C.
Namely, Uzziah, Jotham, Ahaz, and Hezekiah.
The 'minor' prophets Hosea and Micah also wrote during this period.

By the time Isaiah appeared on the scene, the prophets Elijah, Elisha, Obadiah, Joel, Jonah, and Amos had already completed their ministry.
And the state of Israel had been in the promised land for some 700 years.

At this time however the Kingdom had been split into two nations. The Northern kingdom of Israel with the ten tribes, and Judah in the southern kingdom with the remaining two tribes.

By the time of Isaiah's writing, Israel was a tiny nation newly established and caught in the middle of the conflicts between three rising 'superpowers': Egypt, Assyria, and Babylon.
Assyria was poised to overwhelm Israel during this turbulent period of Isaiah's ministry.

Isaiah spoke mainly to the people of Judah – who also faced growing threats from the surrounding nations - and the message was mostly to 'repent' and turn from their wicked ways that The Lord might bless them yet again.

God has tried to reason with them, but they are a 'stubborn people' or 'stiff necked people' (CF 48:4). Isaiah gets his commission in chapter 6 when God asks whom he will send and Isaiah volunteers.

Then I heard the voice of the Lord, saying, *"Whom shall I send, and who will go for Us?"* Then I said, "Here am I. Send me." (Ch.6:8).

Isaiah is particularly concerned with, or focused on, the coming of the Messiah, a savior who will also be a 'light unto the nations' (Ch.42:6).

Throughout this book, Isaiah rages against hypocrisy and the double-dealings of those who would claim to be 'religious' and God-fearing; warning that the Judgment of God is about to descend upon them with a 'consuming fire' (Ch.30:30, 33) unless they repent of their ways.

Notes & Quotes:

It's fair to say I think that the Prophet Isaiah is one of the 'giants' amongst the Bible Prophets. In today's world he would probably have his own TV show! In fact, even in his own day, he was a man widely recognized as being a force to be reckoned with and a definite 'conduit' between man and his Creator.
When he spoke, people listened.

As mentioned earlier, one of the main themes throughout this book, apart from repentance, is the prophecies concerning the coming Messiah. From his lowly birth (Chs.7, 9) to the fact that he would suffer an ignominious death on a cross (Ch.53), thus making himself the perfect sacrifice for mankind's sins, it is all written in graphic detail throughout the book of Isaiah.

Satan Cast out of Heaven

This brief outline of Isaiah would be incomplete if I did not mention chapter 14 of Isaiah – the fall of Lucifer (bright shining one), henceforth referred to as 'Satan'.

How you have fallen from heaven,
O star of the morning, son of the dawn!
You have been cut down to the earth,
You who have weakened the nations!
13 "But you said in your heart,
'**I will** ascend to heaven;
I will raise my throne above the stars of God,
And **I will** sit on the mount of assembly
In the recesses of the north.
14 '**I will** ascend above the heights of the clouds;
I will make myself like the Most High.'
15 "Nevertheless you will be thrust down to Sheol,
To the recesses of the pit."

For those who would doubt this actually refers to the fall of Lucifer/Satan, then the Lord Jesus Himself seems to refer to this event in Luke 10:18 "And He said to them, *"I was watching Satan fall from heaven like lightning."*

The Prophet Ezekiel gives more details on the exalted roll and the subsequent downfall of Lucifer in Ezekiel 28:11-19

Ultimately these writings make clear that the sin of Lucifer that led to his spectacular downfall was PRIDE!

He had become so self-obsessed with his position and power, that he presumed himself to be above even The Lord who had blessed him so abundantly.

Se for instance the 5 - 'I Will's' in the previous example.

Big lesson here – Be careful that you do not let the 'provision' come between you and the provider (The Lord) or your downfall is assured.

King Nebuchadnezzar fell into this trap, and ended up grazing in the field like a wild animal for 7 years!

CF. Daniel 4: 25-36

OBSERVATIONS/NOTES

Jeremiah:

When:
Most likely written during the time of exile, 587–538 B.C.

Who:
Jeremiah the Prophet.

People & Places:
Jeremiah; Nebuchadnezzar; Zedekiah; Pharaoh
Judah; Jerusalem; Babylon; Ammon; Damascus

Sound-Bites:
"Before I formed you in the womb I knew you,
And before you were born I consecrated you;
I have appointed you a prophet to the nations."
(Ch.1:5)

This is what the Lord says: "Let no wise man boast of his wisdom, nor let the mighty man boast of his might, nor a rich man boast of his riches; (Ch 9:23)

"The heart is more deceitful than all else
And is desperately sick;
Who can understand it? (Ch.17:9)

"For I know the plans that I have for you," declares the Lord, "plans for welfare and not for calamity to give you a future and a hope." (Ch.29:11)

This is what the Lord says: "Restrain your voice from weeping
And your eyes from tears;
For your work will be rewarded," declares the Lord,
"And they will return from the land of the enemy." (Ch 31:16)

The Messianic Link:
Messiah is led like a lamb to the slaughter. (Ch.11:19
He will be born a King and descendant of king David. (Ch. 30:9)
Messiah is the 'righteous branch', our Righteousness (Ch.23:5)
He is The Lord Almighty (Ch.23:6)
The Messiah will usher in a new covenant (Ch 31:31-33)

The Book:
At the time of Jeremiah's writing, the Northern kingdom of Israel composing of 10 of the 12 tribes had already fallen to the Assyrian empire when in 722 BC. the ruling city of Samaria fell to Sargon 11 after a 3 year siege.
Jerusalem is in turmoil and the threat of imminent invasion by the Babylonians hung in the air as Jeremiah pronounced the coming judgement of God.

The Southern kingdom of Judah was eventually conquered by the Babylonians under king Nebuchadnezzar in 586 BC.

Jeremiah not only pronounces the coming Judgment of God throughout this book, but also a future restoration of the Kingdom.
This earns him the name of 'the weeping prophet' amongst many scholars.

Judah had fallen far from the will of God, and had sunk into idolatry and immorality.
Jeremiah even describes Judah as a 'harlot' in chapter 22:20.
Even with Jeremiah weeping in their ears, however, warning them to turn from their immoral ways and return to The Lord, they did not repent.

Worse than that, King Zedekiah gave permission for him to be lowered down into a muddy cistern (A pit dug out of stone used for storing water) to shut him up. (Ch.38)

The cistern belongs to the Kings son Malchiah.

By vs 10 the King relented and had him removed after a petition from the eunuch Ebed-Melech.

The final chapters see the fulfillment of Jeremiah's prophecies regarding their Judgment, as Nebuchadnezzar arrives as prophesied to destroy Jerusalem and take the people into captivity in 586 BC.

Notes & Quotes:
Bad news travels fast it is true – but it is seldom welcomed. However, Jeremiah preached not only the

bad news, he also preached the way to prevent it from coming to pass—<u>repentance</u>.

Jeremiah was 'lambasted and lampooned' for his 'message of doom' – but nevertheless he was The Lords messenger faithfully delivering a very unpopular message.

It seemed that to 'repent' or to turn away from their old ways, was just too much of a price for the people to pay.

They could only hear the prophet telling them what they could NOT do, and chose to ignore the alternatives; so they threw him into an old muddy cistern thinking that would be the end of it.

Jeremiah no doubt took little pleasure in the fact that he was finally justified upon the capture of Jerusalem and the subsequent exile to Babylon.

The fact is that it is very easy to give an upbeat positive message to people. High fives and backslaps all around!

Jeremiah gets my respect for delivering a message that he knew was going to be unpopular in the extreme.

Roll on the coming restoration...

OBSERVATIONS/NOTES

Ezekiel:

When:
Between 593 and 571 B.C.

Who:
Ezekiel the Prophet (Ch.1:3).

People & Places:
Ezekiel; Pharaoh; Nebuchadnezzar, king Jehoiachin Judah; Jerusalem; Israel; Babylon; Moab; Edom; Tyre; Egypt

Sound-Bites:
Then He said to me, "Son of man, stand on your feet that I may speak with you!" (Ch.2:1)

"However, if you have warned the righteous man that the righteous should not sin and he does not sin, he shall surely live because he took warning; and you have delivered yourself." (Ch.3:21)

"And I will give them one heart, and put a new spirit within them. And I will remove the heart of stone from their flesh and give them a heart of flesh," (Ch. 11:19)

"I will execute great vengeance on them with wrathful rebukes; and they will know that I am the Lord, when I inflict My vengeance on them." (Ch 25:17)

"Moreover, I will give you a new heart and put a new spirit within you; and I will remove the heart of stone from your flesh and give you a heart of flesh." (Ch. 26:36)

"So I prophesied as He commanded me, and the breath came into them, and they came to life and stood on their feet, an exceedingly great army. "(Ch.37:10)

"I will put My Spirit within you and you will come to life, and I will place you on your own land. Then you will know that I, the Lord, have spoken and done it," declares the Lord. (Ch.37:14)

The Messianic Link:
He is the 'Good Shepherd' in Ch.34:23

The Book:
Ezekiel was one amongst 10,000 Jews taken into captivity by Nebuchadnezzar after a Jewish revolt against their Babylonian overlords in 597 BC.

He received his call to be a prophet when in captivity (see 1:1-3)
Ezekiel begins with Judgment on the house of Israel, and particularly on the leaders of the nation who have been lording it over the common people (Ch.34:1-6).

Idolatrous elders are condemned (Ch. 14) and Babylon is mentioned as the instrument of God's Judgment (Ch.21:21).

In chapter 24 The Lord makes clear to Ezekiel that Jerusalem is under siege and will fall to the Babylonians – and he is not to mourn her loss!

Nebuchadnezzar lays siege to Jerusalem in 588 and by 586 BC her walls were breached and the city looted and burned to the ground.

It was the end of the reign of the house of David, temple worship, and the independent kingdom of Judah.

The book is full of symbolism and allegory as Ezekiel is given visions of the future that include desolation and dispersion to Babylon. The surrounding nations are also to be judged for rejoicing at Jerusalem's destruction (Chaps. 25-32).

Ezekiel finishes with the promise of a final restoration of Israel as The Lord gives him a vision of *'the valley of dry bones'* (Ch.37).

Then He said to me, "Son of man, can these bones live?" And I answered, "Lord God, You Yourself know." **4** Again He said to me, "Prophesy over these bones and say to them, 'You dry bones, hear the word of the Lord.' **5** This is what the Lord God says to these bones: 'Behold, I am going to make breath enter you so that you may come to life. **6** And I will attach tendons to you, make flesh grow back on you, cover you with skin, and put breath in you so that you may come to life; and you will know that I am the Lord.'"

Notes & Quotes:
Ezekiel was indeed the 'man of the moment' as God placed him amongst the exiles to show that He was

not only God in geographical Judah but, indeed God over all the Earth.

It was a revelation to the people that they could still worship God, even without the Temple in Jerusalem itself. The Lord made that clear, when he instigated the ministry of Ezekiel after he was led into exile with the rest of them.

The institution that we now know as the Synagogue began in Babylon, and this played a huge part in keeping the nation together whilst they were in captivity.

Sometimes, just when everything seems lost, The Lord will indeed show us a way forward.

As an aside…Followers of the cult movie Pulp Fiction will be more than a little familiar with chapter 25 and the 'execute great vengeance upon them ' Samuel L Jackson plays the hitman Jules Winnfield and largely mis-quotes this verse before executing his victim.

Interesting how the media often misquote or quote out of context the Bible when it suits them…just sayin'

OBSERVATIONS/NOTES

Daniel:

When:
Around 530 B.C.

Who:
Traditionally attributed to the Prophet Daniel.

People & Places:
Daniel (Belteshazzar); Hananiah; Mishael; Azariah; Nebuchadnezzar; Darius; Gabriel.
Judah; Jerusalem; Babylon; Persia

Sound-Bites:
As for these four youths, God gave them knowledge and intelligence in every branch of literature and wisdom; Daniel even understood all kinds of visions and dreams. (Ch.1:17)

As for every matter of wisdom and understanding about which the king consulted them, he found them ten times better than all the magicians and conjurers who were in all his realm. (Ch.1:20)

"The king answered Daniel and said, "Surely your God is a God of gods and a Lord of kings and a revealer of mysteries, since you have been able to reveal this mystery." (Ch.2:47)

"But *even* if *He does* not, let it be known to you, O king, that we are not going to serve your gods nor worship the golden statue that you have set up." (Ch 3: 18)

"…..For He is the living God and enduring forever,
And His kingdom is one which will not be destroyed,
And His dominion will be forever." (Ch.6:26)

"I kept looking
Until thrones were set up,
And the Ancient of Days took *His* seat;
His garment *was* white as snow,
And the hair of His head like pure wool.
His throne *was* ablaze with flames,
Its wheels *were* a burning fire." (Ch 7:9)

"Seventy weeks have been decreed for your people and your holy city, to finish the wrongdoing, to make an end of sin, to make atonement for guilt, to bring in everlasting righteousness, to seal up vision and prophecy, and to anoint the Most Holy Place." (Ch 9:24)

Then he said to me, "Do not be afraid, Daniel, for from the first day that you set your heart on understanding *this* and on humbling yourself before your God, your words were heard, and I have come in *response to* your words." (Ch. 10:12)

But the prince of the kingdom of Persia was standing in my way for twenty-one days; then behold, Michael, one of the chief princes, came to help me, for I had been left there with the kings of Persia. (Ch. 10:13)

"But as for you, Daniel, keep these words secret and seal up the book until the end of time; many will roam about, and knowledge will increase." (Ch 12:4)

The Messianic Link:
Messiah is the 'Son of Man' (Ch.7:13-14)
He is the stone that smashes the kingdoms, and the everlasting kingdom (Ch.2:34, 44)
He is the fourth man in the fiery furnace (Ch.3:25)

The Book:
This book follows the visions and ministry of Daniel after he has been deported to Babylon by Nebuchadnezzar.

The first chapter begins with the appointment of Daniel and his three friends, Hananiah, Mishael and Azariah, into the royal court of Nebuchadnezzar and taken on as 'wise men' or advisors to the king.

In the second chapter Daniel interprets a disturbing dream that Nebuchadnezzar has, thereby leading to the promotion of Daniel to Chief Prefect.

Chapter 3, however, sees Daniel's three friends (re-named Shadrach, Meshach & Abed-nego) thrown into a furnace for their refusal to worship the golden statue—only to be saved by God and the 'fourth man' in the furnace with them.

King Nebuchadnezzar acknowledges 'Daniel's God' in chapter 4, and goes mad for 7 years according to the Word spoken by Daniel.

Chapter 5 sees Nebuchadnezzar's son, Belshazzar, and the passage relating to the writing on the wall that Daniel interprets correctly to prophesy the end of Belshazzar's kingdom.

In Chapter 6 Daniel is thrown into the lion's den by his new ruler, Darius the Mede, but God closes the mouths of the lions and he is unscathed, and promoted by King Darius.

The last chapters are all prophecies and visions relating to the 'end times' and in particular the time of 'Tribulation', a period of seven years of turmoil to come in the last days. (Ch.9:24-27)

Notes & Quotes:

This is a complex, and at the same time exciting, book. We have Daniel and his friends appointed as leaders over a nation that enslaved them, the escape from the fiery furnace and the escape from the lions' den, perhaps the most well-known of the stories, as well as Nebuchadnezzar's 7-year-long madness! (Daniel Ch 4)

This is also a most popular book for the students of eschatology (studies relating to the end-times), and rightly so as the last 5 chapters are dedicated to the 'End Days' and full of allegory and visual stimuli as to just when it will all occur, and what we can expect to happen.

Along with the book of Revelation in the New Testament, this is a major book for anyone interested in the tribulation period, and just exactly where the Christians will be when it is happening!
Are you pre, mid, or post tribulation? That is the question!

Pre-Trib = Christians will be raptured before the tribulation begins.

Mid-Trib = Rapture is in the middle of the tribulation period of 7 years.

Post Trib = Christians will have to go through the tribulation period and be gathered together at the end.

The whole rapture issue is filled with controversy and opinion. Many believe in it, and many do not.

I for one am a strong believer in not only the rapture or 'taking away' of the Church, and also an advocate of the pre-tribulation theory.

Why? In a nutshell. The tribulation period is a time of Gods wrath & judgement upon the people of the Earth.

To put Christians through this 'wrath & Judgement' period would be to again punish Christ for the sins of the people.

This would in effect be to nullify the sacrifice of Jesus on the cross – a sacrifice that was made 'once and for all' (c.f. Hebrews 10:1-18).

Unthinkable!

We are no longer 'children of wrath' (1 Thessalonians 5:9) but are instead 'the righteousness of God in Christ' (2 Corinthians 5:21).

There are of course many more arguments to support the pre-tribulation stand – However I trust that this will be a good start to any debate on the subject...

OBSERVATIONS/NOTES

Lamentations:

When:

Most likely written during the time of exile, 587–538 B.C.

Who:

Anonymous but largely attributed to Jeremiah the Prophet.

People & Places:

Jeremiah

Judah; Jerusalem; Israel

Sound-Bites:

How lonely sits the city

That was full of people!

She has become like a widow

Who was once great among the nations!

She who was a princess among the provinces

Has become a forced laborer! (Ch.1:1)

Arise, whimper in the night
At the beginning of the night watches;
Pour out your heart like water
Before the presence of the Lord;

Raise your hands to Him
For the life of your little ones
Who languish because of hunger
At the head of every street. (Ch 2:19)

Restore us to You, O Lord, that we may be restored;
Renew our days as of old, (Ch.5:21)

Those who used to eat delicacies
Are made to tremble in the streets;
Those who were raised in crimson *clothing*
Embrace garbage heaps. (Ch 4:5)

The Messianic Link:

The Messiah is captive (Ch.4:20)

The Book:

Originally named 'Ekah' meaning 'how' or 'Alas!' the name reverted to 'Lamentations' after being translated as such in the Septuagint – the Greek translation of the Old Testament.

Lamentations really carries on where Jeremiah left off, and continues to mourn the loss of Jerusalem and the extent of the punishment that The Lord has put upon them. Jerusalem is laid waste, its people either captured or killed.

In chapter 4 we see the depths of depravation that the siege had brought them to, as it reduced them to the cannibalization of their own children.

The book begins by lamenting the fate of Jerusalem and its people but by the middle of the book, centres on the goodness of God.

He is the Lord of **hope (3:21,24-25)**, of **love (3:22)**, of **faithfulness (3:23)**, of **salvation and restoration (3:26)**.

In spite of all the hardship endured, "The Lord's acts of mercy indeed do not end, For His compassions do not fail.
²³ *They* are new every morning; Great is Your faithfulness. **(3:22-23)**.

Near the end of the book, faith rises from Jerusalem's lamentable condition, to acknowledge The Lords eternal reign: "You, Lord, rule forever;
Your throne is from generation to generation." **(5:19;**

Notes & Quotes:

Lamentations is full of mourning for the people of Judah and the city of Jerusalem. The fact is, however, that the people repented after the event; a bit like saying you're sorry only because you have been caught!

Throughout the book of Jeremiah, the Prophet warned them what was to come if they did not turn from their wicked ways; and in Lamentations we have the inevitable result when they refused.

Orthodox Jews customarily read the complete book of Lamentations aloud on the ninth day of Ab, the traditional date of the destruction of Solomon's temple in 586.

The Roman catholic church traditionally read this book over the last 3 days of Holy Week.

The book of Lamentation does exactly as the title suggests – mourns and laments the fate of rebellious Jerusalem and its people.

Yes indeed. God is the God of many chances—he is also the God of the last chance!
■■

OBSERVATIONS/NOTES

OBSERVATIONS/NOTES

Other Bible Summary eBooks By This Author

Minor Prophets Summary: Spotlight On The Minor Prophets: Bible Study Guide - 12 Book Bundle (Old Testament Prophets Study Guide)

******

Made in the USA
Coppell, TX
26 May 2025

49883780R00024